A Restricted View
From Under The Hedge

(In The Wintertime)

This Belongs To

....

....

....

Published in the UK by
The Hedgehog Poetry Press
5, Coppack House
Churchill Avenue
Clevedon
BS21 6QW

www.hedgehogpress.co.uk

A CIP Catalogue record for this book is available from the
British Library.

ISSN: 2515-9313   ISBN: 978-1-9164806-8-1

WELCOME

Welcome to the fourth issue of Arfur, which marks the end of the first year of the Hedgehog Poetry Press (if you ignore the phoney war of the few months of panic that lead-up to the first publications.)

In many ways, it has gone rather well. We have had some incredible poets in the four issues of this wee magazine, and by the time you read this will have also published eight single poet collections, two *Conversations*, four anthologies, 20 Sticklebacks, oh and sent 100 of our Vapour Trail pamphlets on journeys around the world (or to Basingstoke and back) gathering some great poems on the web site as they get passed from poet-to-poet.

Obviously, it has also been a complete shambles at times too – I think teething troubles are the technical name – and I am slowly getting things straight in my head about how to make it all work, so I will apologise for all of the issues and hope to do better in the future.

As for Arfur, I feel it needs a change if it is to be sustainable and so this is very much the end of something and I have to go away and think it all up again as future issues will look and feel a bit different, but then everything needs dreaming-up again here and there if it isn't to become stale, so we will just have to see.

I hope you like this issue.
Mark

Poems from,

Reviews

The Poems

CHRISTOPHER LEVENSON

Code

Years it took them at Bletchley in the Second World War
to decipher the Nazi code, to elicit meaning
from seemingly random numbers and letters.
But at least they knew what they were looking for
and the cost of failure.
 When entering the board rooms, country clubs and homes
of those you presume are friends, nothing's as simple
as morse or semaphore: a quizzical raised eyebrow
from an old school blazer and tie, a deferential
smile in the face of authority, this is the minimal
acknowledgement of someone
who's 'not one of us', an outsider.
A nod and a wink, a shoulder turned away,
a special handshake, pat phrases falling in place,
an accent noted, a wrong address, and you
are filtered out.   It cannot be learnt,
this international language, no grammars exist:
you read between the lines.

Neutrality : a footnote   (May 1940)

A British official's diary entry for 4th May ::
"Home at eight. Dined and worked.
Planning conquest of Iceland for next week.
Shall probably be too late!
Saw several broods of ducklings."

When neutral Denmark fell to invading Germans,
Iceland, land of the Viking Sagas, but also the site
of the Althing, the world's first
democratic parliament, might have been next.
Britain reacted haphazardly :
under Colonel Robert Sturges some new recruits,
seven hundred marines, not even equipped with rifles and many sea-
sick,
were cramped on board the HMS Berwick and HMS Glasgow,
took firearms training on deck, With few maps, mostly poor,
one drawn from memory,   and no one knowing the language,
they came ashore before dawn at Reykjavik,
met no resistance, arrested the German Consul,
disabled communications,, commandeered vehicles,
occupied radio stations, landing areas,
'to secure the North Atlantic" and maintain
the naval blockade of Germany

Though Iceland's official neutrality lasted till war's end
it was not observed by the occupying troops:
British, Canadians, Yanks found many of Iceland's women
open to truce, or more. Some came back with them
to the New World, They leave us picturing
alternative histories.

Cell

As movers reduce our living room
to bare necessities, walls stript
of prints and paintings,
I watch canyons build
around us. Encircled by cartons --
Cedar Creek, Absolut Vodka,
Pimm's Number One, London Gin --
a lifetime's supply of bottled euphoria
but destined for other gullets,
I gaze around soberly
at all the cardboard orgies,
the late night party's abandon,
tearful drunken farewells.
and see myself become
reluctant anchorite.

LUCÍA ORELLANA DAMACELA

Longevity River

Body rafting
a white ghost jumping
out of an unfinished song
the sound of distance

Round rocks under my feet
fossilized eggs
brought back to life
by the rapturous waters

My locks aquatic serpents
as I claim horizontal this river

*

Water
is a good answer to fire
but this one
is probably undrinkable

I assume mud and detritus
as well as bustling colonies
about 60%
of their DNA same as mine

Runaway life slightly disoriented
by the new geography

*

It is only fair
to break a sweat
and pour it into the fresh water
the salty taste diluted
Almost immediately
as easy as it sounds
within this barely figured
gargoyle of my reflection

I also build an appetite
with planks from a fisher boat wreck

*

Red in the water
it could be a cut in my almost numb toes
traces of scarlet ink
intense first and then diluted

A highly saturated red hue
is obtained by crushing cochineals
a bug from these lands
their bodies lost to the cause of art

Blood on the other hand
is not a reliable pigment

*

Sometimes my body aches
before the rain
sometimes I let
minute fish nibble at my feet

Gorging on my dead skin
their tiny eyes looking my way
like breastfeeding babies
their hunger pains gone

Sometimes I let rain
swallow me whole heal me

*

It is called
Longevity River
it robinhoods minerals and energy
from the mountains

to share with us mortals
Buoyant my body
greedy for life I let it
spread like water hyacinths

I stay beyond
the recommended time

*

There is a path from here
and it goes towards a place
with hot meals and car horns
but I have learned how to return

to these swirling versions of wholeness
just in case I fill my bag with stones
no to mark the way
but to ground this moment

Memory
is a powerful yet frail time machine

ALISON JONES

Make it Stretch

When things are pulled tight like a drum skin,
and the singing tension can almost be felt,
you have to play to the negative spaces.

She called it a treat. A secret language,
hatched from a jar or gifted in fine paper,
snug in cupboard dark, the common dialect

of sweetness. Lumps stiff as communion dresses,
newly starched and waiting for someone to hold.
Sprinkled, fingers furtive between flotsam and crumbs.

Sifted from the air, a fine thing to offer up
with lamp lit tales, beneath rose framed windows
of home; eaten while watching for tall clouds

like winding sheets, lifting at the edges
to reveal the moon's hard white face.

CEINWEN E. CARIAD HAYDON

A Right Jobsworth

I'm sewn into this job now.
'Sir, you've had a little girl,
you must be made up.' Made up?
if only they knew. 'Right,
let's get on you lot. Parabolas.'
I want to travel, write,
and take risks on mountains –
I'm sewn into this job now.

Twenty-seven faces stare
at the blackboard all,
except brainy Bridget,
bored out of their minds.
Like me, they want to be
doing something else,
be someone else. Dream on.
My phone vibrates,
a sackable offence.
I glance at another photo,
the thirteenth today.
I'm sewn into this job now.

Mary, grey with spent
ecstasy, eyes bright with love
for our daughter
cradled asleep in her arms.
Arms that once clutched me
hard when she came, shuddered
in our sweet marriage bed,
in the forest, on the beach.
At twelve, before I've had a bite
a text, lightened with emojis,
don't forget the nappies, no kisses.
I'm sewn into this job now.

JOHN F. DEANE

Ballet

In the plum-blue out-there darkness and high above the intently-watching
mountains – the slow ballet of the galaxies;

and can you sense the fissures and glaciations down the faces of the
planets that are, up there, in the dance, serene?

I am at home with heather-tuft and turf-bank, with curlew-call and the
constant love-nothings murmured to the coast by the soft-capped waves.

There is an old fragility in the lace-like edges of all things, and how the
solitary hawthorn (with its invisible, roseate angels, its prickly littlepeople)
is shot through with ivy and the wild dog rose.

Tonight the constellations will appear in another quarter of the sky, my
bones will sear with sentience of seasoning, of now, of geologic time.

And I would share in the gentle communion of saints, as the quizzical
light the moon has focused on the lawn will be gone by morning, the
masterful trail the fox has left through the grasses will vanish soon,
flushing the world warm with memories of its golden ochre light.

Fox

Mid-morning quiet in the townland; the postman has gone, glissando, by;
delivery trucks have been and even the lapdogs who fancied themselves
as wolverines a while, have fallen still.

I have settled in a patch of meadow, to pray in a rustle of longing towards
my God but winds of the world come whistling through, and the myriads
of branches in my mind's deep woods hustle noisily.

I know how my Christ stays watchful as a fox, biding time; how love will
touch each falling raindrop, each circling satellite, each far-out hurtling
galaxy, every crash and ping of the cosmos – while I circle that still and
clamouring point from which all things take being;

but, like Job, like Job I have made covenant with him, he will know my
ways, will number all my veins, will harvest my desires.

And the ocean rumbles nearby and the sand-grains shift and fall.

SHEENAGH PUGH

The Joy of Five

The death mask: wax and plaster
and living clay
that follows the man's indents,
his scars and furrows,
that makes him eye us sideways,
still grave and worried
after five hundred years,
as who should say:
to bring the dead alive, my dear,
to bring the dead alive.

Then the plates, the paper,
the silvered film
where the latent image seems
to swim from nowhere.
They call it a likeness, this inch-tall
man who can neither move
nor speak. It is what character
comes to: what else will serve
to bring the dead alive, my dear,
to bring the dead alive?

It was cinema said "action",
get up and walk,
gave the voices back
to folk long gone.
What would Andrew Marvell
say, to see years speed by
in time-lapse? Maybe
"Now make it stand still".
What brings the dead alive, my dear,
what brings the dead alive?

23

Bodies have been frozen
in vaults, loved pets cloned,
(they say a cat's markings
are never the same twice).
But loss knows no reason;
none so alone
as the bereaved, so ruthless:
they will try anything
to bring the dead alive, my dear,
to bring the dead alive.

A man in Dorset hands
a wife only he can see
into a cart; talks, all the way,
to the void at his shoulder.
The space where someone was,
the gap of light
between the bare branches:
hold on to that.

ANDY BROWN

Mister Hielz

The day was Divisions and Spellings
When our teacher told us, *'Children, stop
What you are doing now and pay attention.
This is Mr Hielz.'* The sallow stranger
Wore a suit that even my grandfather
Would have taken to the charity; a hat
I'd seen in some relation's history books.

' You, you and you,' he said mechanically,
Picking out his victims in what seemed
A purely random manner. Those of us
Who'd had the finger pointed, stood
Awkwardly and shuffled through the door,
Not knowing where we headed to or why,
Feeling *their* eyes on *our* backs as we went.

In the soundless room behind the library
We stared at the reflections in our shoes.
'This...' said Mister Hielz, *'is Mister Violin
And you will follow and obey him well.
He'll be a friend for life if you work hard,'*
His foreign vowels and consonants
Meaning we only half heard him...

And only half-understood *what* we heard
As he slathered the horse-hair with rosin,
Shouldered the rosewood and conjured
A Slavic reel that held us mesmerised,
And keeps us spell-bound decades on,
In the preparatory tuning up of orchestras;
The ghostly loops of fiddles in subways.

DEBJANI CHATTERJEE

February Fun

Savoury
or sweet,
tossed in air,
stuck to the ceiling;
pancake.

Haiku

The eyes of children
shine with anticipation.
The future beckons.

Dear Ma, Your Face...

Dear Ma, your face is a landscape
on which I see Guwahati where you were born,
Patna where you were schooled,
Kolkata and Chennai where you went to college,
Mumbai where you dipped your toes
in the sea, Delhi where you married ...
All of India is traced upon your beautiful face.

Dear Ma, your face is a landscape
that played peek-a-boo in childhood games.
It carries the passport and visa stamps
of Indonesia, Japan, Bangladesh, Hong Kong,
Egypt, Morocco, Poland... so many
exotic places that you made home for me;
so many memories drawn on your loving face.

Dear Ma, your face is a landscape
I never tire to gaze upon,
the first face after the midwife's
That I saw through tears in Dadu's
Bungalow No. 3, Timarpur Road, Civil Lines.
Your face gave me my precious family;
all our ancestors live in your age-etched face.

Dear Ma, your face is my endless landscape;
the flowers of love glow on your tranquil face.

Five Clerihews

John Montague, Earl of Sandwich
Enjoyed roast beef between bread slices which
Allowed him to stay gambling at a late-night session.
When he died, doctors said, he had suffered from indigestion.

Rabindranath Tagore
was a poet, philosopher, artist, and more.
When his critics praised him, it was no surprise;
he knew they were mesmerised by his Nobel Prize.

George Gordon, Lord Byron
was a rakehell siren
who reveled in seducing both lords and ladies of the nobility,
not excepting his own half-sister Augusta Leigh.

Ada, Lady Lovelace
Gambled and lost at every horse race.
Though the world's first computer programmer,
She never discovered an algorithm to pick a winner.

Edward Carpenter,
Socialist writer, philosopher, gay activist, and traveler,
was called 'cranky' for his ideas and lifestyle
but was much loved by the very same rank and file.

ARUNDHATHI SUBRAMANIAM

The Bus to Ajmer

We're a circus troupe of a kind,

sixteen Pakistanis, one Indian,
juddering away
on a bus to Ajmer --

twelve men, eyes kohl-rimmed,
one beside me, his body rigid

with conviction, gaze itinerant
with desire, eyeing

the breathless woman from Islamabad
whose conversation is unstoppered, damp

with a sadness she isn't aware of,
in front of whom bobs and fumes

a self-proclaimed fakir,
all costume and comic despair,

waving wild hands at
Sunny bhaiyya, stolid tour leader,

father of four, our circus ringmaster,
accountant from Lahore.

And sitting by the driver,
the Karachi poet,

his speech softened
by Charminar cigarettes

and all the old confusions,
        achingly familiar.

Politesse is abundant.
I welcome them to my Indian saint,
they welcome me to their faith.

At the shrine the twelve men unwind
into malangs,

whirling slowly
into a place
of studied ecstasy

that is suddenly,
                jaggedly,
        a kind of abandon.

The fakir sings,
the poet fidgets,
Sunny bhaiyya prays.

There is some envy in our gaze.
Excluded briefly
from the euphoria,
the sad woman and I
close our eyes.

We are a circus still
at the end of it

but cooled by marble,
heated by song,

    quieted by the tale
of yet another madman

caught up in a sandstorm of love
lurching down to Hind
from distant Persia
in a blunder of fever and instinct
that some call mission,

our disguises are just a bit
askew,

bodies more provisional,
stories less italicized,

    breath more rationed,
    certainties more unlaced

(as the old Khwaja,
crazy vagrant from Sistan,
    might have wanted).

    The poet and I exchange addresses.

The strange thing about love

is that it melts you

into an amateur,

never again a professional
                        even
                            on the subject of yourself.

*

The strange thing about love

is that you disagree,

disagree wildly,

and then figure it's wiser

to dance.

*

The strange thing about love

is that it evicts you
from the land of echoes
you thought was home

and leads you to
friends

sitting
under the stars

in ancient
bewilderment.

C.C RUSSELL

Augmented

You wake up. There is a sun low on the virtual horizon, perfect god finger light stretching through the thin clouds towards you. It's the beginning of your story. You have a past, of course, but that isn't important at this immediate moment. What's important is that you are separate from it. What's important is you are standing here, on the shoulder of a highway. There is an inconsistent sort of traffic passing you by. There is this sun, there is a city far in the distance shimmering like a mirage of pixels. It's hot but you don't feel it, not really. You hear the cars pass, a voice occasionally yells out from an open window as they go by too quickly to hold on to. It's your story from here on out but it looks like you only are given one direction to go. And so you walk. You pick up your feet and walk with the traffic towards the buildings, towards this purple sun. This is the beginning, this is your story. As much as you can make it.

Closer Than They Appear

I remember you as stretches
of expressway, as lights
sparkling and fading in the rearview
mirror, illuminating my own reflection
in fits and shudders.
I remember you as what I wanted
you to be, what I tried to be for you.
I remember you as a game.
I remember you as anything
but a game.

HANNAH BROCKBANK

Acanthis

Unlike Acanthis
who was transformed
into a thin-boned bird
to save her from grief,

my marred chalk throat
no longer trills
between the white rust
of crucifers, chickweed
and sow thistle.

In my silence,
you may mistake me
for stone dead,
but still I alight
on your rounded stomach,
but take flight
before I'm felt.

Bowl Barrow

A Bowl Barrow is an ancient burial mound shaped like an upturned bowl

Don't close your eyes,
the anaesthetist says.
He taps the top of my hand
like a blackbird pecks the ground
to raise worms in the rain.

My mouth a well of words -
I say I can feel
the anaesthetic's cloud drift
towards my heart,

I say, I'm floating
over the mound I climbed as a girl,
and that curled inside it was a boy,
his hands wrapped around the neck
of a collared urn,
waiting to collect life,

I say, when I was five,
I'd put my ear to the barrow's side
and heard the boy turn, and press his fists
against its sides,

I say, how I'd feared
the boy's muddied hands would burst through
and grasp my throat until
my life spilled out.

Moving

I'm prone to moments like these,
when I lose hold of my senses
at the end of a rope-swing,
and think I can fly, or,
when galloping through woods
with my eyes closed
until the whip
of small branches
snaps me back to sight.

And then, at the edge
of the jade lake,
I think nothing
of distance or hypothermia,
or who'd care
if the water claimed me?

Only when I'm half way across,
and my pale limbs barely glow
in the black-green silt,
does terror swell inside
at the thought
of chasms,
the inverted Pyrenean mountain
under my body,
the aching cold
of geological time
creaking up between
my arms and legs.

Only then, a voice swims
through my mind
and tells me
to keep moving
moving moving.

Glass Fish

Every week
after your birth,
I buy a gaudy glass fish
until I have a shoal swimming
mouth to tailfin
along my paperless desk.
Each one is born
from a flux of fire,
sand, arsenic
and drawn out breath.
Their hollow-bright bodies
flare and set on fire
their spattered sides
of coral, amber, and teal,
each fin and gill
a full drop of milk-glass,
their wide thick-rimmed mouths
a venting of light.

PIPPA LITTLE

Dreaming Alaska

We were just driving around. Late in the evening
but still light. Some nights it never got dark,
down at heel motels and apartment blocks,
junction boxes, the perfumeries of refried fats.
someone I almost called a friend
had sent me an email: *This gives me a giggle
every year. The usual ritual. Dreaming Alaska!
Thought I'd pass it on to you.*
I looked at the image in the car. Your car was old,
the upholstery smelled of toffee, I leaned my cheek
against the glass. No relief from twilight.
Her son's blonde, pink-faced, shy before her camera.
He kneels, a gun slim as a furled umbrella in one hand,
the other grasping an outspur of the biggest antlers
I've ever seen. It takes me a moment to understand
the head of the creature is still attached,
looking straight at me. An odd dark seeps out of his skin.
I recall grainy black-and-whites like that,
evidence of séance. For nights afterwards
I am crazy, restless and itchy in my skin,
can't sleep so we drive and drive for miles.
Looking back, it was someone else
caught sight of the back of her head in the slanted mirrors,
saw the dark hole in the bone of everything.

CHARLES WILKINSON

The Impersonal

A pitch of regret concealed in soft wind
& the duplicity of weather, neither winter
nor summer: pale radiance, the gold skimmed off.
Distance the key when stealing without hands:
stings remotely contrived in a different land.
 With no width of daylight to work, what robs
is virtual - blind theft: a site's fakery, its stolen
 nouns & colours & always a request to click;
an art of anonymous raiding, face without face.
 Yet hours are spent homesick for fingers
in the pocket, the time when theft was touch:
 flesh closing on the leather wallet; the crime
in a known street; the victim passing by under
a broad, unambiguous sun & soon the cry
of loss when shadows slipped off at sly noon.

Attachments

The formation of an attachment
was then no document summoned
from the files, but love's first sign
expressed in black italic, the bold
script slanting & forward, the last
line inscribed with a flourish, hope
flowing through the suitor's hand.

Delivery was slow, horseback
or penny post allowed no instant
ardour, though anticipation sowed
the prospect of delight..

                    Unsealing
released the words that travelled
the distance, & a fragrance of
another place; her perfume rising
from the page.

               An open attachment is
now odourless: without smell of sea
in the day's ambiguous surf; cursors
should hesitate for there's no way
of telling what danger is delivered
with a paper clip.

              Think of the usurpation
of nouns: how strangers can hide
in the names of friends:
                  a click on the link
creates a world of worms & ransomeware.

The day here is the longing
for life beyond the signal, alone with
the forest & logged off: free from
the keyboard, ascending like a saint
above high branches' dwindling green
& onto the troposphere, where storms
turn the wheels of light; the view below
is of clouds that hold no information
in a curved rim of sky around earth:
the last of air shaped to seal the blue.

JEN ROUSE

The Depressive's Blues

. . . but also the therapist must recognize . . . that the experience of the other is, in the end, unyieldingly private and unknowable.–Love's Executioner, *Irvin D. Yalom, M.D.*

I.

Tell me this isn't true.

Help me. Understand. Why death
is sinking in again. Pulling for two
clean weeks of breath and being,
only to end in something stirring
the same indigo pit of pain. I don't
want to be here with the women
I cannot have, their petulant men
looming in my shadow; with the family
I don't want, ringing my heart like a soggy
washcloth--all the cleaning of wounds
rewarded with guilt gritty as sand.

These poems are so bland, so bland.

Help me. Take my hand and walk me away
from this place. I glare out the window
at the fields folding in, at the core
of a city. What could I possibly say
to make this new?

II.

Tell me this isn't true.

She is back. In pale robin's egg linen
and sunglasses, she greets me at the door.
The arms I enter pull two clean weeks
of breath from me once more. I cannot
allow this, and yet I smile and tell her
she looks like an old movie star.

For hours I listen, the diligent,
silent companion, to the woman
who takes my rapture and turns on it:
"If you really loved me," she hisses,
"you would stay." I provide the pedestal,
rich mahogany gleaming in light, and I provide
the fall. I take. In the giving, the plummet
so great only one man knows how
far and what it means to land like this.
Scarred.
                    Beside her willow-step, I cannot be
lovely; I cannot override the strides she will take
to insult my life without her. Isn't it evident, she insists,
she always knows best when what is mine is ours.

III.

Thus I may advise, argue, badger,
cajole, goad, implore, or simply endure,
hoping that the patient's neurotic world
view will crumble away from sheer fatigue.

Crumble me. I am broken already,
and for
so long.

IV.

Sunset. The sky curls yellow, plumes
pink, and I cannot take a hand, or hear
applause. I am responsible for what isn't
true, and no matter if I engage you,
these poems are so bland, so
bland, and blue.

MAGGIE MACKAY

Mellon Udrigle

Waiting for you, unannounced, beyond a high moor, is a tinkling name
on a road with no number, a secret, secret of dolphins, whale

and the occasional sheep; beyond the dunes, Camas a'Charaig's stretch
of snow-sand strokes your feet, and there at the gloaming, be seduced by

the sea of liquid gold. Midas would envy you this treasure trove of elements.
Your eyes will pop at views of Suilven, Coigach, An Teallach, Gruinard Bay.

Here rests a place of sea mist and shimmer, ever-changing, every moment,
a place where fairies and kelpies might just make magic.

where you find only a few cottages, caravans and a telephone box,
beauty to dream away the day. Wheesht, it's a secret.

Clean Air

When I was young, coal fires in every room,
my mother grafting at the grates,
shuttles and bunkers, pokers and tongs,
and still, in Mjanga, charcoal and wood,
girls beachcombing the road at first light.
Afghan bukhari and sandari, drum and pit
fuelled by animal dung, harvest dregs,
burning little feet, burning many hands,
fuelling headaches, toxic kitchens,
young lungs wasted, blasted lungs,
and now, wind energy clean as Highland skies,
ten turbines bedded in the Sound of Jura canyon,
acid rain no more, lichen-loving pure air,
greenhouse gas-free at last. Somewhere renewed.

A Lead Mark in a Box

*

Witness women scrub sweat out of cotton
by the Nankokwe's current rush through forest,
while the men brew beer, take shelter in the shade.
*

Harriet, kitchen maid at Linthouse Mansion
scrubs tatties, heaves jelly pans.
'I work hard six and a half days a week.
The words 'rights' and 'votes' fill my waking day.'
*

Segregated by the male vote to a separate seating area
at the first World's Anti-Slavery Convention of 1840,
Lucretia Mott calls to us through the centuries
"I long for the day my sisters will rise,
and occupy the sphere
to which they are called by their high nature and destiny."
*

My dear wife's place is at home.
A gentlewoman,
she does not possess
the capacity to make such choices.
Parliament would be a ruin.
*

Esther Roper went out and about,
to Manchester women in factories and at home.
'Women pay taxes, contribute to the economy.
The least men in Parliament can do is give you a vote,
and a say on laws affecting your working conditions.'
*

Helen cracked the whip. The Royal Albert Hall saw
burly men hurl themselves on me,
smother my mouth with their coarse hands,
carry me bodily and with violence.
Lies in the press and Lloyd George's disdain.
*

Woodrow felt an icy breath on the back of his neck,
thinking about the 1912 election, not exactly a landslide,
and if enough of the four million women voters
- and maybe some of their husbands or brothers -
turned against him, he might lose in 1916...
Maybe it was time to talk to his colleagues on the Hill...
*

In 2017 a Bolton woman was asked
Will you vote in future?
I really don't know.
What is certain though,
is politics is going to have to get a hell
of a lot more interesting
if I, and my girlfriends, are going
 to put a cross in a box.
Emily Davidson falls under trampling hooves.

A Study in Moments of Tolerance

I thought a present was for keeps.
You stand on the top rung of the ladder,
six feet or more in your bare feet.
No eye contact, you ask for it back
change your mind
with a more deserving woman in mind.

I'm flummoxed, unable
to say yes or no in the hall,
Out of nowhere you voice this request.
I send it weeks later in the post,
glass in frame, splinters and cracks.
*

You gave me the best Christmas present another year
'Adventures in Form'. Your hidden depths.
A potholing expedition to the cave formations
inside your head. Once, the hand-blown glass
I chose for you, indigo, beautiful,
recycled back to me. Oops.
Unspoken to this day, a tear in my soul.
*

Falling out of earth's orbit
my marriage sucked into outer space
you take me in, for forty-eight hours
I sleep with cat claws dug deep
into high shelves, feline wanderings,
brain fug, my body more flight than fight.
Helsinki. Coffee houses.
You retrace your marriage. Exhaust me.
We never speak with such intimacy again
Chalk, chalk, cheese, chalk...
You hearing impaired, me a bletherskite.

*

A note beside the power socket.
after the house clearance,
remember to return the timer.
I leave it behind.
This must be how your brother feels,
not that I've met him.
Who taught you unkindness?
*

New Year's Day. Debts cleared.
Pyjamas, 10 am. Half your permed head
emerges through the living room door
That bridging loan. The interest.
Families don't pay each other interest.
A broken start, an irritating scratch
suppurating sore. *Send me the bill.*
*

Mum stands at the window,
waves at the ghosts of Christmas.
Those must be the most selfish people in the world.
I take the hit as their Audi slips into memory,
south towards the M6. Four hundred miles
*

You stand in a room as if it is the wrong room.
Sullen is the name of the room mist.
Busy is your preferred state of being.
Then nothing can be snatched away by the stepmother
- wooden spoon beatings on livid calves.
*

We give you a teddy bear on your sixtieth birthday
No one should go that long without their own Teddy
Mine is ear-torn and stitched, a Merrythought treasure
I walloped him across hand beaten carpets,
write him into poems. He's family.
Maybe soft toys are the difference?
*

Gaps, fissures, stunted growth
you call my mother *Mummy*
for the mother you reclaim from infancy
who died the year I was born.
*

Mum reminds me, you've got to remember
not everyone was brought up like you.
We don't know
what childhood's been like for other people...
*

Twice a year, on your whistle stop-drop-ins
you ride the jobs to do-merry-go-round.
I edge between your thinness
and the high bare wall in Mum's kitchen.
We might be teenagers
after a fall out about nothing
we can even understand, mumbling in segments.
You sit down to EastEnders. I write in the front room.

JOAN LENNON

His Nets

Long after the village was empty,
he still climbed the sharp slope
behind the shore
to tend his nets.
No rain on that coast.
No streams down the hills.
No wells.
"I learned it from the birds,"
he used to say,
when there was someone there to tell.

He'd seen them sip
the drops of fog
condensed, one by one,
onto cactus spikes
and lichen threads.
He'd set his nets upright on the hill
and let the sea wind
herd the shoals of mist
into their mesh.
Funnelled the drops,
one by one,
into his bucket.
Carried it down the hill.

"I learned it from the birds,"
he'd say,
when there was no one there to ask,
"What birds?"

JENNIE E. OWEN

Love Poem

Love poetry is a fraud I will not commit,
sugar on the tongue, sour on the breath.

I am not a greetings card spewing
shredded doves into the rain.

I have heart, I concede, the bloody type
pumping and pushing fleshy mechanics,

not sentiments.

To list your endearing qualities,
(of which there are many),
would simply bullet point my faults,
(of which there are more).

Poetry can tie us up, can hand grenade a heart.

(I would sigh my last breath for you).

My Professor

You rub your hands across your face,
the roughness of your stubble, the tiredness of your eyes.
A crease across your forehead,
the fluidity of youth, setting.

My Professor.
corners of your mouth turned down.
Eyes on your half empty glass
suspended, like a cheap trick
above the table
Words squeal on the rim, and I say it again.

NATALIE CRICK

devil at sea

the sea was shaken
awake by the devil
crouched on her chest

he spoke
through laced lips
into her throat

as she unrolled
her wet mouth

he became the hot
breath
that touched her

slowly

vexing her watery words
to a tragic drone

his breathing softened
like sheep meat in teeth

gently gnawing the icy tips
cavities listening
with nothing inside

bodies shattered
against terrible reefs

he watched her
until the sun rose

patient and small
but growing

noiselessly
on the cusp of a wave

One day, and the next

they melt
fall as severed limbs
hold daylight
beneath layers of ice.

They seek cover
paint their eyes shut
bleed into plastic bags.
They lick their wounds
with salt tongue to ease sickness.

Half-resurrected
they still and float on their backs

to stare at the sun
with quiet faces
in a more refined stupor.

Others drip like bones
hanging from twine in some barnyard:
a land of freshly dead.

The knife does not see
the wound it makes,

the evolving tide of murder.

Vessel

My house is a ship that has long departed,
the white sails cast adrift.
Withdraw from the skin and let the bones cool dry.

I hang in the back room
marinating in myself,
left out for later.

My little daughter
pulses in our dark kitchen
waiting like an old dog counting a storm,

her face a thin moon
haggard in solitude,
jaws wide open.

IMOGEN FORSTER

Bittern

We have heard the boom, the sound
of air blown across a bottle's neck,
and now he steps out into the sunlit
channel, hunched, deliberate, dressed
in the browns and yellows of a soldier.

Bent on fishing, head drawn forward,
feet splayed on warm mud, he watches;
stabs at small silver things that come
glittering up, and swallows them.

Oblivious of the crowd gathered
in the dusty wooden hide, he stalks
back into his reedbed. We gasp,
laugh out loud together, clap
our hands at the gift of such a bird.

Flowers of Sulphur

The skewed logic of this dream
has brought me to a place where
I am to rehearse mourning.

C is sick but she still runs.
Her soles slap unforgiving stone,
sweat running under the scapula.

Now there's a jump-cut
to funeral wreaths, the breath
and death-stink of lilies,

the indelible stain
of pollen, the revelations
of dye on a glass slide.

She speaks of the peritoneal
arch, the unappeasable
cells that are consuming her,

that have become her twin,
her inseparable double.
But here is her lavish mouth

as I wake, breathing the deep
scents of her hair, her own
glittering stupendous crown.

Bestiary

We are on a beach in Oman
and among the tide's dry litter
I find the lantern-skin of a boxfish,
salt-cured, standing on stiff fins
at its four corners, prehistoric limbs.

Now it's Torridon in April,
chilly, the unsteady boulders
difficult to clamber over,
our poles all but useless.

Above us a pair of ptarmigan
are pecking among smaller stones.
Plump, clownish, they are still
half winter-white, half in their
mottled summer camouflage,
the male with his scarlet eye-flash.
Feather-warm in thin sunshine
they feed companionably, undisturbed.

Fish and bird, the consolation
of what's well-remembered.

ANDREW GREIG

The Scales

She wrote a fair few
poems in her lifetime
They weighed next to nothing
on worldly scales

Small wonder
she was dour

Yet when she had her say
the planet creaked from its abyss
till the bright and dark pans
were dead level

Her words must have been
much heavier than they looked
or our world
that much lighter

PAUL WARING

Roots Of Obsession

At first
little more than an itch
bluebottle persistent.

Not until by turns
tendrils thread
a pernicious rash

sap-ready
to take over like ivy —
and lava leaks

from urge-filled tap
will you know —
this is just the start.

After Her

he stood statue-still.
A stopped clock
locked inside stares —

windowless eyes
unable to see a future
beyond rooms
whose walls
clung tight to the past.

Everyone would tell him
in time you'll be ready
to face the world

rescue garden from grief
dead-head flowers
let in linnet's song
watch first light
ripen into a smile.

But he knew
already
there is too much time.

CHERYL PEARSON

The Net

Here's what I remember:
the muscles in my forearm bunched
so tight against the weight, my mermaid

flexed and sweated with the stress,
so her green ink took on
the sheen of sickness.

I was ready for the wealth of living light
to rave across the deck. The flipping
glitter and flash of the fish.

What I wasn't prepared for was this:
a woman slung in the net's scoop,
pale, silent, stripped to the waist.

I cut her free with my fish knife,
saw her flinch at the wink of scales
on the tip. The sealskin

pooled around her shins.
I ask you: what would you have done?
I'd never have found her like on land.

I unwrapped her in the morning sun.
Golden, she was. Mine. I gave her
my shirt. I took her hand.

First Snow

I wake knowing the world has changed – I don't know how. You
follow me out of sleep in increments, the way
a city skyline blinks on in the evening. Light by light. I wonder what

dreams you have piloted. Heads next and next
on the pillows, flickering like film-reel - I was flying, and then I fell.
And now it's morning, the ceiling's full

of a strange light, and I turn the blinds to find the sky has fallen too,
during the night, has laid itself down
in shuffled softness on each house, each street. A printless,

luminous white. The world altered entirely while we
slept, our mind's lights spinning on. Look: a bird on the gentled
fence, trying his notes in a strange land. And there,

a string of ice ringing under the roof. All the light of the sky belongs
to us now, for these few hours
or days while the cold keeps. The alchemical thrill of it – all that

light from all that dark,
like the swoop of an owl at night from nowhere: a flurry of wings; the
flame of a single feather, falling.

PENELOPE SHUTTLE

purpose of the window and the door

light takes pleasure
in the windows

the outdoor library
cherishes its twiggy book

the kitchen
lets sleeping dogs lie

roof himself would be sorely missed
but here he is
blooming like a red flower over us

the doors are quietly here   and there

the architecture can take care of itself
says the architect
so long as the building smells right –
mosquito nets, tatami mats, and moonlight

Church of the Crayfish Christ

Someone is singing
by leaps and bounds
on her happy way
to church
in the parish of Lyonesse
where men and women cling
to the helping hands of music
and when Our Lord The Crayfish Christ
sings out his sermon
to our listening ears
we the congregation understand
everything for the very first time

Beloveds
you must live for pleasure alone!
This is my gospel
Am I not half-brother to the moon?
Are not the deeds of my claw everlasting joy and delight?

Alleluia and Amen!
Praise to the Crayfish Christ Our King

From: Lyonesse: a book-length sequence, work in progress

72

Boat-drawn

Not a word I say
counts
in this boat-drawn city
where no one cares
if I live or die
which is good for me
to take on board
the world does not revolve
around me
as I was often told as a child
nor does it owe me a living
and in this full-blown boat-drawn city
I can only murmur from street to street
how true   Lyonesse   how true

From: Lyonesse: a book-length sequence, work in progress.

73

PETER J. KING

Remember Me

"a Swiss company [...] will compress and super-heat your loved one's cremated ashes and turn them into a man-made diamond that can be worn and cherished."

cremate, then
sift the ashes,
cleanse them with hyssop

and when they are clean,
when they are pure as
the wing of a collared dove,

with fire and pressure,
heavy heat transforming,
become

       radiant
       princess
       round brilliant
if this be madness,
shine on

GEOFF HATTERSLEY

Cap Detention

You were put in a uniform
for the first time in your life,
waved off to boys' grammar school.
Part of the uniform was a daft cap,
to be worn like a flag of surrender
from leaving home to arriving at school.

The '60s were not a great time to be alive
in short trousers till the age of thirteen
and a daft cap. Even so, you could write
Mothers of Invention on your satchel
and ridiculous as it now seems
this was a rebellious act.

Prefects were stationed at odd parts of town
and if you were caught with no cap
you'd be given cap detention,
an hour of writing
'I must wear my cap when travelling to and from school'
over and over.

You're reading a poem

Lovely poet
is an oxymoron

he said, I've never read
a book of poems

that failed to make me feel
like smacking the poet

they use the word like
like it's a mantra

and the one thing
you can be certain of

is that what they make out
something is like

is never like what
they make out it's like

and that's how you know

The Effort

He wakes slowly
from a dream of childhood,
a dream of strength
and a sense of purpose,
a dream full of wishes
that might come true,
plans for tomorrow
and the day after.

He sits drinking water
and not smoking a cigarette
at three o'clock in the morning.

He once stopped for two days
but it was a mistake –
he ran out of money
in a hostile city -
had to hitch a lift back,
making small talk
as his head spun
from the effort of not smoking.

He sits scratching his chin
and not smoking a cigarette
at four o'clock in the morning.

The guy behind the wheel
had said, *Howdy, partner,*
I'm from Austin, Texas,
and started banging on
about armadillos,
whose vile eating habits
include a taste
for maggot-ridden flesh.

He sits tapping his fingers
and not smoking a cigarette
at five o'clock in the morning.

DEB SCUDDER

The Boiling Playground

The bug is massive, trundling across the playground.
All the children gathered for a look.
I wish they would leave it be and carry on playing
but they continue, for far longer than is sensible
and I get caught up in it. They won't let me go
and find out how damp the sandpit sand is today,
by squeezing it between my fingers.
I liked it just damp enough to hold a shape,
but only for a few seconds, because I also like it to crumble in little lumps
that I can rub like flour and butter in a bowl.
Falling, dry between my digits is unacceptable,
as is forming a tight ball wet enough to leak a mess when constricted.
It was a huge black beetle. We didn't know what type.
Small bodies circle, boys growling at each other
about how ferocious its pincers are and none of them daring to touch.
The girls watch wide-eyed, sometimes shrieking, trying to back away,
grasping each other's arms. No small hand on my arm
but I'm held nonetheless and carried along, following the beetles slow progress.
The sun is a laser super-focused where my parting is, and they won't let me go.
All I want is to not be near bodies.
I get jostled along, a moment of silence in a symphony of voices.
It's the incessance that does it, the egging on and the squealing,
running away and then immediately coming back, unable to resist
the beast, magnified in tiny minds to the danger and wonder of a tiger.
We traverse the concrete, the beetle and us,
and it all goes on for so long that in the end I have no choice.
I rush forward and stamp on the beetle as hard as I can,
hear it crack, feel it crunch under my heel, but not quite flatten
smooth to the ground as I wanted it to.

It's a dead huge beetle now and its innards spew
like chewed liquorice over the concrete.
The children are disgusted with me,
but the sand is perfect today.

The Sea

I'm forced into the orange corner slanting with sea glass.
I lie on my front and imagine large male hands pressing into my back.
There has been too much death.

Commonly known as a misspelled lie.
Commonly known as stoicism,
it's the wall of a tidal wave, approaching too fast.
It needs to scatter itself on the rocks to oxygenate.

It's the lamb trapped in barbed wire I rescued,
not caring about my gloves being snatched away,
the drizzle making my fingers slip. Not noticing
the gouges in my jumper, just reaching
for the tiny strong firmness of it.

It's the child's impotent fury at being held and giggling
and having no power at all to escape.

It's the sea sloshing at my feet, trying to pull me in, teasing,
Come on in! We're having a party, just a small get together, it'll be fun!
I stiffen and move away, along the train tracks, away from the boozy air.
There is too much of it, voices, people, and then another person dies
and the ocean flips, cracking over my head.
I don't drown but stand blank, dripping salt from my fingertips.

For a long time afterwards there are still droplets in my ears,
reminding me of the flood.

JULIAN TURNER

If Buses Die

then this is where they go, to Boisdale, Uist,
where the metalled road breaks up in Machair,
the low sun chandeliers the shattered glass
in tortured frames which falls as molten rain,
a screen where films of long-gone journeys show,
an Odeon for an audience of air:

that charabanc that choked us all the way
to Formby, its seating glossed to a slick by bums,
and brindled by bubblegum, its hard nylon
and squalid antimacassars, the bone-thick drone
of the engine deafening and drowned insects
floating in condensation and fag ends;

the Magic Bus we caught from Amsterdam
to Greece, an Alexander-bodied Leopard
so clapped-out it took a fist of steel
to make it go, a dark fortnight of the soul,
our heads like melons numb on strangers' shoulders,
friends who lasted half-way round the world;

from Ouarzazarte to Marrakech, stuck
in a Saviem beetling across the High Atlas,
its carapace of luggage bright, its front-end
on hair-pins swinging out over ether,
all of us sick, the Berbers laughing and hens
catwalking the aisle, leggy, cosmopolitan.

All buses come here some day, rotting down
to metal, glass and blasted rubber tyres,
bedding down in flags and boggy reeds,
the late sun squinting up, highlighting them,
their luminous shells as constellation points

A Sonnet Struggles in its Chains

So, what's it going to look like, our new world?
A scattering of star-bright tax-free states
joined up by streams of pure liquidity,
extracting all wealth from the muddy globe,

capillaries of precious metals safe
from you and me, yet leaching minerals
from all soils so we cannot feed ourselves.
It sucks up cash from each unsanctioned source,

however small, then moves across to feed
on living souls, downloading surplus from
the next bunch, in the sunny Surrey hills.

And are we going to take it lying down,
like carcasses the maggots eat from within?
When do we start the New Jerusalem?

JACQUELINE SAPHRA

The Jealousies

I wake hourly to the knock of blooded shoes
ascending the wooden stair to my chamber.
They speak from wet sole mouths, say again
and again that they are mine and must be
admitted; they creep into my bed, tuck
their stilettoes under my chin, lever wide
my lips, press their toecaps into my tongue
and drool for my confession. By my silence
I refuse to call them mine, so they turn
and stamp their heels into my chest until
my ribs open to expose the meat, my lungs
burst into green song and my heart is cleft.

Sunrise and Swag

'... over and over again we have seen that there is in this country another power greater than that which has its seat at Westminster' Clement Atlee

The river sings a duet with the mist
as gulls gavotte around the overflow
and peck at City scum; two Freemen row
across the dawn, five plastic bottles drift
seawards. The river's left the beach undressed
again. A dead rat pitches to and fro
on green-fringed ripples. While the tide is low,
mudlarks mob the shore at hope and sift
frisking the sand for swag, and as the sun
slides pinkly in to light up bankers' reach,
a host of windows seize the light. The gods
command the brokers' choir to rise as one
and sing a song of money: the plundered beach
is deafened as the trading floor applauds.

MIKE FERGUSON

Wind-Powered Sun

Conversion is the link in interdependence. Off-grid, wind wanders where the sun does not shine. Hybrids take Nature to new highs in inbreeding. Ships that sailed the Nile were powered more by prophecy than moving air. Downdrafts that churn are energy hallucinations of sunshine burns. King Lear in his madness cracked open the moulds to new technologies. Uneven heat on roughness and rotation blows and blows and blows. An Aeolian harp shines too / meets gods above hills where sound is light powered by the wind.

PAUL STEPHENSON

Getting What You're Given

It was usually half an hour before
my father got home from work.

My mother would arm herself
with a plastic bag and take off

her apron, step into tall black
Wellingtons, a sheepskin coat.

End of the lane, she'd ring on Reg,
goad him out with a few coins.

Trowel in hand, they'd climb
all the way up the muddy peat

incline of his field. Then he'd stop
and he'd stoop, legs like an easel

and bend, tug hard at the roots
of whatever she'd in mind boiling.

Chernobyl, April 1986

My mother was obsessed with radiation –
nuclear fallout, kitchen microwaves.

She would reheat her mug of cold tea.
'Don't get too close' she'd say. One day

walking back from school across the rec',
the week of the explosion in Ukraine,

we got caught out with no umbrella.
Convinced of acid rain, concerned ill winds

had blown our way, she ordered me
and my brother to run ahead, ordered us

to wait in the bathroom til she came up
to Head 'n' Shoulders our schoolboy scalp,

or was it Timotei? In turn we bent forwards,
face-down in the basin, tap spouts digging

into the nape. Lather, rinse, lather, rinse,
with whatever the immersion could muster,

we screwed our eyes tight to stop them stinging,
blind to events fifteen hundred miles east,

the slow brewing of Glasnost and Perestroika,
in that accidental era of Gorbachev and Thatcher.

Epithets (Mother and Son)

Good, I'm a kiss-smotherer, arms-right-round-wrapper,
table-setter, up-and-dry-washer, scum-ring-rinser, bins-out-putter,
a without-being-asked-hooverer, place-looking-tidy-keeper,
in-this-house-do-as-I do-doer, Ps-and-Qs-minder, nicely-asker,
a going-to-be-back-late-caller, out-of-trouble-keeper, down-knuckler,
low-volume-turner, socks-up-puller, reviser, smiler, behaver.

Bad, I'm a wave-maker, boat-rocker, cat-among-the-pigeons-putter,
apple-cart-upsetter, insult-to-injury-adder, fuel-onto-fire-pourer,
a there-till-its-gone-sitter, sleeping-dogs-won't-lie-letter,
havoc-creater, abuse-spouter, always-for-a-fight-looker,
to-me-like-that-how-dare-you-talker, me-too-far-this-time-pusher,
a black-kettle-pot-caller, point-misser, back-chatter, agro-giver,
to-your-father-if-you-don't-like-it-speaker, door-slammer, it-lumper,
round-the-bend-up-the-wall-doolally-driver, the-last-say-haver.

Mum, she's an on-with-things-regardless-carrier, on-soldierer,
along-jogger, chin-up-keeper, through-muddler, stuck-right-in-getter,
a duvet-shaker, pocket-checker, sock-darner, cushion-plumper,
it-like-it-is-teller, if-I-do-don't-minder, if-you-don't-you-cry-laugher,
a blessings-counter, pinch-of-salt-things-taker, on-it-sleeper,
bright-side-looker, wood-toucher, finger-crosser; she's a future-worrier.

The original title of this poem was 'The It-Lumper and the Cushion-Plumper' but perhaps this only makes sense once you have read the poem, hence the simpler title.

The Spanish Language Student

The first Sunday at breakfast, he came down dressed.
We kicked off. Plied him with bacon and eggs, sausages,

mushrooms, baked beans, fried bread. We obliged HP.
Then thick white rounds of toast. He had to try Marmite.

And lemon curd. Then our turn. We watched him pick up
his knife, spread sugar from the bowl onto buttered toast,

which he cut into triangles, ate between sips of milky tea.
It was THE most outrageous, brilliant thing I'd ever seen.

At dinner, Mum dished up, said, *Careful, it's extremely hot!*
He asked, *Please, what it is?*, and flicked his well-thumbed

bilingual dictionary pages after we said, *is typical English,*
you like it, is very famous, very delicious, is toad in the hole.

Ambre Solaire

A week in the sun, Majorca, 1981.
The hotel lived up to the artist's impression,
except breakfast: hard white bread rolls,

strawberry jam in plastic portions, and Mum
creeping food into under-the-table bags –
It's criminal for them to go to waste.

The morning shopping for a decent knife
and forgetting getting flip-flops. A picnic
on the beach, waiting in trunks in turn

for hard white bread rolls and Spanish cheese.
Then Mum cutting through her little finger,
seeing it hang like a raw chipolata.

I don't remember the screams. We were told
to stay put. I can see Dad lead her away,
her legs like pink blancmange over burning sand

up to the hotel clinic for her stitches and jabs.
She said she chatted with the doctor, practised
It's raining (*está lloviendo*), not knowing *It's sunny.*

That holiday. The one where she severed a nerve
and my flippers and mask lay on the sand,
spattered with blood and protection factor.

GRAHAM ROOK

Needless Poem #69.4

I heard that song
where you claimed that
you wrote a poem. A
poem that lived on the
face of a desiccated
morsel from a *Winalot*
bag. You never
explained why it
mattered so much that
my Alsatian turned her
nose up at it, although
with contemplation I
think therefore I see. I
didn't want to be an
Instapoet or to *slam* or
live anywhere other
than on a page and
perhaps that is true of
you too. We never
really spoke of these
things whilst you were
my Mother, butcher or
window cleaner, my
ailing *dramatico* sock
drawer dictator, but
then it was only ever
your smile that spoke
to me and that never
bothered your eyes.

ANNA SAUNDERS

Ghosting For Beginners

Some people must have a lot of time on their hands, was the uncharitable first thought I had when I received a copy of Anna Saunders collection, *Ghosting For Beginners*. I mean, she already runs the Cheltenham Festival, seemingly coming from nowhere before turning it into one of the most interesting – cool – and dare I say prestigious Literary Festivals of them all? But then she has time to write a book of poems too, her own slim volume.

What can I say, perhaps I let my own default sloth colour my thinking sometimes, I'm not proud to admit it.

So, in truth when I opened, the rather lovely looking book from the indefatigable Indigo Dreams, I wouldn't say I was hoping not to like it, but it was going to have to work a little magic to win me over.

And that is exactly what it did. In truth, I should have known better, I mean I have read Anna's work before and always been impressed, but even by the standards she clearly sets herself, this is a superlative collection of poetry. Because Anna Saunders is a quite exceptional poet, she creates worlds with the minimum of words and there is a depth that goes way beyond what you initially think is her subject matter. It is *that*, which is the most impressive part of all. Anna has this rare ability to conjure up complete and deeply rich stories of life, family and place with such a small number of words, it constantly blindsides you and she is the very definition of a poet that nags at the edges of your brain long after you think you have finished reading her work.

I caught up with Anna, to apologise for being a fool and to find out more about her book and the festival.

The first thing that strikes me about GFB is that you have an obvious love for words - their placement and weight is always perfect. Who and what do you feel created this love in you?

"Firstly - thank you very much. I was lucky enough to be born into a house of books. My parents (journalists/novelists/poets) were both avid readers and I inherited that. I have always devoured books - mainly novels and poetry - and I love the way good literature can excite and inspire. I have learnt so much from reading Great poets and novelists - studying form is the best way to develop as a writer."

Who in terms of poetry was the first writer to catch your imagination and make you think it would be for you?

"I think I first fell in love with poetry when I read Dylan Thomas - it was an old tatty copy of his poems that I found in a charity shop. I loved the sepia tint of the dusty pages and the lush musicality of his work. I didn't entirely understand every line, but it affected me - I felt the electric charge of his words."

Have you still got any of you early poems and how do they stand-up now?

"I was about 7 or 8 when I first wrote poetry - I've lost them, but still have some of the poems I wrote as an anguished teenager. And I daren't read them again."

A lot of your poems seem to pack a film's worth of story into them and have real echoes of the past. I'm thinking something like 'Befriending The Butcher.' Do you set out to write that way consciously - is it a fiction - or is it a case of sharing a memory?

"I think poetry can be very cinematic and can tell stories in an economic and potent way. I am very interested in writing modern narrative poetry as you have observed! Befriending the Butcher is based on a true story; sometimes real events have all the poetry you need. This poem celebrates the life of my dad's pal Ken - who looked like a rugged Thomas Hardy character and ' spent his days dressing flesh/ preparing Primal Cuts and his nights –carving wood,/ reading brick-heavy biographies of Larkin or Keats.""

You have a real talent for observation - the people in your poems definitely come to life as you read, which is odd as a lot are ghosts ;o) - and you seem to love the people you describe. Do you 'collect' people in your everyday life, magpie-like or again, is this a detailed imagination at work?

"It's a mixture really - sometimes I create a 'cast' to illustrate ideas, perhaps use myth or legend, or sometimes the persona of the poem is real - or a thinly veiled version of myself. Many of the ghosts in *Ghosting For Beginners* are real - people from my past, or places, experiences that haunt me - some are fictional spectres, brought ' to life' so I can explore themes such as guilt - for example in On How Ghosts Take the Moral Highground, where the protagonists' dead lover hangs over her bed ' shroud bound, glassy faced, righteous' ..'like a see -through falcon, ready to drop on prey'"

I love the humour in your work, it is really dark, does that often get you into trouble?

"Ha ha yes - it can also go unnoticed. One friend described a poem as 'too dark' when I thought I was using black humour!"

Can I ask you to give a brief description of two or three of the poems in the book?

The Lapwing

"Myth has it, that a maid was turned into a lapwing for stealing scissors. But this poem condemns those who judge other for petty sins. ('You caught her stealing, your punishment was to cast her to the sky'). The poem addresses the idea that none of us are perfect, or without sin and if we pretend to be, we will be haunted by guilt.

' We cannot escape our sins/they hang feathered above us/
and even when we sit alone, in silence
their plaintive song echoes in our ears'"

The Ventriloquist Dolls of the Dead,

"Have you ever seen anyone with the same mannerisms as someone you have lost? My dad died a few years ago and since then I have been haunted by the sight of others with his grin or gestures. I imagined these partial doppelgangers as Vent Dolls
' wooden faced with ennui/ suddenly jumping into life and flashing you that smile'"

The Ghost Marriage

"This poem was inspired by the chinese ghost marriages - an astonishing tradition in which men, or women could still marry their intended, even if their fiancé died before the wedding. In this poem the bereaved has a rooster stand in for her husand at the ceremony - a common ritual. -
The poem begins
Finding himself in the afterlife without a wife
he thinks of his earth bound love.
How curse he was to die
only days before his marriage."

If I can ask a couple of questions about the Cheltenham Poetry Festival - Why would you decide to start such a thing - doesn't it take over your life?
"Many of my projects begin with an impulse, a gut feeling that I should do something. That was how Cheltenham Poetry Festival began. Quite a few people told me not to do it, that it was impractical and I wouldn't get funding etc - but I am a bit of a contrarian, and felt strongly about devoting several days a year to poetry events - so I steamed forward!"
It seems to have grown this year, what are your aims for it in the coming years?
"Audience figures have grown nicely in the past few year and last year doubled by 100%! There is a real demand for the highest of the literary forms with more people reading and writing it than ever. For 2019 year we are going to expand on our success and brig even more class acts to Cheltenham as well as celebrating local talent."

Are you worried that it will get in the way of your writing?
"Yes, it does. It eats my time - though is worth it in the end - when the 'poetry party with a healthy dose of anarchy (The Guardian) kicks off!"
Who were the poets this year that made it all worthwhile and who would you love to be booking for next year?
"Our 2018 Festival ran for a full 14 days and our jam-packed programme celebrated the power of words in a programme of exciting live literature events. Highlights of 2018 include BBC Radio 6Music's Poet in Residence Murray Lachlan Young - 'A rock 'n' roll poet of our time' (Chrissie Hynde), 'Chap hop's leading exponent' (The Wall Street Journal) Professor Elemental, Salford rising star JB Barrington, hip hop artist TrueMendous, 'the missing link between Jarvis Cocker and Roger McGough' (Irish Times) Vinny Peculiar, internationally acclaimed writer Amir Darwish, ex judo champ turned poet Owen Lowery and TS Eliot Prize winner Jacob Polley.

As ever we welcomed some of the UK's most important contemporary poets to the stage. They included Jonathan Davidson, Martyn Crucefix, Sam Willets, Costa- Prize winner Jonathan Edwards, Rishi Dastidar, Pat Borthwick, Gill McEvoy, Peter Raynard, Tom Sastry, Wayne Holloway Smith, Cora Greenhill, Adam Horovitz, Jane Commane, Chrys Salt, Rachael Allen and Patrick Mackie.

I do have wish list for next year and am steadily building a programme. We'd love to invite Andrew Mcmillan, Ben Zephaniah, Carrie Etter - and we do have some great names pencilled in. Perhaps I can come back in a future magazine and tell you more?"
We really hope she does!

Anna Saunders' *Ghosting For Beginners* is available from www.indigodreams.co.uk

MARGARET ROYALL

A Review of the poetry of Kerry Darbishire

I first met Kerry, an accomplished, prize-winning poet, on a creative writing retreat on the mystical Isle of Iona. Her stunning poetry written in the landscape impressed me and made me long to produce such well-crafted verse myself. Shortly afterwards her first poetry collection *A Lift of Wings* was published by Indigo Dreams. I bought a copy as a Christmas present for my poet son, who was equally charmed by her writing. Naturally I read the book first myself!

I next encountered Kerry at a Lakeland writing retreat at Rydal Hall in Cumbria. The group was granted a private visit to Wordsworth's home next door, Rydal Mount, where she read an award-winning poem seated on Wordsworth's couch. In turn we were permitted to sit in his writing chair by the window, all hoping to imbibe a little of the Wordsworth magic.

Recently Kerry's second poetry collection has been published *Distance Sweet on my Tongue*, which I immediately acquired. The cover is charmingly illustrated by her artist husband, Stephen Darbishire. Her writing is imaginative and authentic with many poems themed around the people and places of her beloved Cumbria. Reading the poems we are transported there and the Cumbrian landscape comes vividly alive. She has a gift for succinctly capturing the essence of a place, a time, a person with an economy of elegantly chosen phrases, using juxtaposition of words with a fresh perspective, delightful on the ear. Her work has been described thus:

"These poems deeply rooted in Cumbrian ground, grown over with a cornucopia of mosses and flowers, but which reach out to the wider world. In her attention to detail, Darbishire presents a landscape and community moving to their own timeless rhythms. The poems are heady with scent and colour, guaranteed to be sweet on the tongue." Polly Atkin

I would highly recommend you acquaint yourself with Kerry's accomplished writing. You will not be disappointed.

KERRY DARBISHIRE

Distance Sweet on my Tongue

Kerry Darbishire is perhaps the perfect English poet, although these days I'm not sure if that is still taken as a compliment however much it should be. Her work here is centred on her beloved Cumbria and she has a painterly eye for details that the rest of us would miss or disregard, an ability with very few words to create a sense of time and place that few possess and an intense devotion to the nature around her that allows her to develop the theme of family and characters that matter to her, or at least once did.

There is a genuine music in her words that goes beyond her often critical eye, and this allows her to go beyond a reporting of nature and dig into the people that clearly have caught her attention – never judgemental, but curious, not critical, but observant, you feel that she misses nothing, but is happy to let the world go past without comment.

And for me, that is the strength of the collection and Kerry's poetry generally. This quiet knowledge of the world that is hinted at by action rather than opinion and allows her to move beyond the nature into other areas, is Kerry peeling the onion of the world.

I was really pleased to talk to Kerry about her work.

When was the first time that you knew you wanted to write poetry - who inspired you?
"I wrote my first real poem when Donald Campbell tragically died in 1967 on Coniston Water. I was so shocked and saddened I wrote in response and because the local magazine, Cumbria published it, I felt I perhaps could write some more. I've long lost the poem, and maybe that's a good thing!"

101

Who would you say has been the greatest influence upon your work?
"That's difficult to answer because there are many poets I admire and inspire me to write because I'm surprised by what happens somewhere in their writing, some magic and I can't put the poem down. There are too many wonderful poets to mention but: Jack Gilbert, Dylan Thomas, Billy Collins, Sean O'Brien, John Burnside, Elizabeth Burns, Esther Morgan, Pascale Petit, Liz Berry and Judy Brown, who mentored me in 2013 at the Wordsworth Trust. All very different, all wonderful."

Reading 'Distance Sweet On My Tongue,' I thought at first there was a sadness, a melancholy about the collection, but as I have read (and re-read) it, I think I began to realise that there is a quiet strength in your work and perhaps that it was something quite different. Looking at it now as a finished book, how do you see the collection as a whole and what does it mean to you?
"I would like to think of this collection as a celebration of my encounters. I'm happy to share the happy and sad times – that's life. Though I admit writing sad poems seems easier than happy ones! I've always been fascinated by time and its passing and trying to get my head around the strength and fragility of existence, how people come in and go out of your life, the taste of it, how it's affected me and others. I think this is the essence of my new collection. But I guess the readers will decide."

But are you happy with it - did it do its job?
"It's when someone tells me they've enjoyed and can relate to my poetry, that I feel I've made a connection and know it's done something I set out to do."

You have an obvious love of nature - what influenced that as you were growing-up?
"Yes, I love and respect all nature. I grew up beside a river (well mostly in a river) in the Lake District and spent all my time playing outside in the woods and fields on my own making up games, watching water, weather, animals, belonging to the landscape, so I guess the smells and rhythms of my surroundings sunk in deep."

The book feels like a long journey where you are visiting places you love or loved. Did you set out to tell a story with the collection?

"I tend to draw on the people I've known, loved, places I've been, experiences throughout my life, especially songs because they remind me of where I was, how I felt, who I was with at the time. My childhood was filled with music and made a huge impression on me to the point I wrote pop songs during the 80's and 90's. Perhaps I was always wanting to tell stories in some form. In the words of Tennessee Williams, *In memory everything seems to happen to music.*"

Speaking of music, (tenuous, I know) I always think with that artists/bands split between those that write songs and those that think in albums. With poets, I'm always curious about their focus too, how they come to have a book of their work. Do you think in terms of writing individual poems and bring them together or do you plan a book, give it structure and then write to fill it out?

"When I begin to write a poem I'm not thinking where it might go or fit in, that comes afterwards. It was only after I'd written over a hundred poems, I began to see what was going on and thought they would make a collection. Having said that, I have an idea for a small collection, so I've kept some poems back that might possibly fit into a new pamphlet."

In your poetry and in life, do you see yourself as an outsider, an observer rather than a participant?

"I'm not sure how to answer this, I observe, I remember, I make notes which is a solitary thing until I start to bounce the ideas and lines around on the page, become more involved and curious. Like songwriting, it sometimes feels as if writing has a life of its own."

You have a real gift for rich, painterly - layered - description. Is this something you have worked at to develop or was it always there?

"Well that's a lovely thing to say, thank you. I wanted to go to art school, be a painter, always wanted to transfer my feeling/responses to paper so perhaps I satisfy this with a pen/keyboard! But I've had to work hard at this, reading, listening to different forms of poetry knowing I will never stop learning."

The collection feels very personal, family members are mentioned throughout, is it a case acknowledging parts of your earlier life or just remembering?

"I had a very eclectic upbringing. Our house was constantly filled with writers, musicians, artists, vagabonds, climbers, and the rest! I think that was the start of my interest, wanting to understand people from all walks of life, it seemed important, to the point I wrote my mother's life story, Kay's Ark, which included these interesting people who'd slept under our roof, not only as a tribute to her extraordinary life but because I was curious to know more about her, what made her the way she was. It felt like I was writing out a very long poem!"

The beautiful painting on the cover is obviously by your husband, have you ever collaborated beyond that?

"Funny you should ask that. My husband, Steve has painted all his life and now we are thinking about writing a book together, a combination of his paintings, my poetry and many years spent on a fairly remote fellside here in Cumbria."

Can I ask you to give a brief description of two or three of the poems in the book?

"The poem Rooted is about a midden, which is a household dump before refuse was collected, and situated near the house. We found one here when we first arrived and dug up this beautiful cup, it felt like a door into someone's past, like treasure, lucky, perhaps a good omen. Edward's Stable is an old stable you might come across in an abandoned farmstead, full of old ways, where you can imagine the horses, the harvest, the couple who farmed the land. We have such a stable here. Like the Moon is about my mother who sadly had Alzheimer's towards the end of her days. I write to honour the important things."

What do you have planned next?

"Apart from collaborating with my husband, I'm planning the pamphlet I mentioned earlier for my father who suffered from PTSD after WW2, who was misunderstood, appeared and disappeared throughout my early life. It's only now, decades after his death, I'm attempting to understand his perspective and write it down. And as I'm addicted to writing poetry, what else can I do but carry on trying to make sense of ideas and words in the hope I will reach readers in some way."

Kerry Darbishire's *Distance Sweet on my Tongue* is available from www.indigodreams.co.uk

SERENA MAYER

Talking to Jonathan Stubbs

Serena Mayer is a new voice in the poetry world. Her strange texts are like towers of building blocks assembled by a child, uncentred and unstable, all edges and angles, with remnants of punctuation throughout and a total lack of anything except thematic linking one line to the next for the reader to initially focus on. Each poem is a kind of impressionistic ladder that the reader has to slowly climb, poetry without epiphany or closure, although occasionally the last lines such as 'part of the story of being' ('New Histories') or 'together in another order' ('Apparition') feel like a kind of summary or key to what has gone before, encouraging re-reading and reconsideration. Mayer's first book, *Theoretical Complexities* is published by Broken Sleep Books.

You don't give much away to the reader, but your brief biography states that you 'studied anthropology and social geography, and [are] interested in hidden texts and forgotten or discarded language.' Can you unpack that a bit? What's it got to do with poetry?

"I am very interested in how society works, how it leaves traces of itself, organises itself, excludes and includes, and how it occupies the spaces it lives in. I love the fact that, for instance, people make their own paths across the corners of parks and waste ground instead of following the prescribed routes. I came to see these as secret routes, personal mappings, of places. In cities, of course, it can be described as psychogeography, but that seems a very urban, male discourse. There are historical sites and traces of people everywhere, of course. In fact this summer's unseasonably hot weather revealed many forgotten or unknown sites and markings across the UK. Of course, tied up with our knowledge is the matter of how we use it. Claude Lévi-Strauss was a fantastic anthropologist but indulged in some questionable assumptions and ideas about the 'savage'. Ideas and contexts change, although academia doesn't like those who go against the grain or indulge in different systems. The Pitt Rivers Museum in Oxford, for instance, exhibits material by type of object rather than by country of origin. I think it's fantastic to compare, say, an African cudgel with a British policeman's truncheon, but many specialists do not."

And the poetry?

"Sorry, I am getting to that. The different ways of dealing with material, with objects, and people's own use of place, made me think about hidden maps, hidden texts. I am fascinated by the historical and literary interpretations of ancient texts, from archaeological sites but also the literal fragments of Sappho, and the slippage involved in translation, depending on the translator's concerns and skills.

Somehow this led me, via the idea of the reader making what they will of what they read, to the idea of hidden texts within other texts. Secret texts, forgotten texts, codes, thrown away language (the rubbish on the street, unread or abandoned books, half-heard songs from cars passing or open windows) to seeking out my own texts within the work of others."

So your poetry is simply, or only, constructed from other texts?

"That is my writing process at the moment. I choose phrases or excerpts from books I find and build my poems, line by line. The horizontal placing of each of the lines is dependent upon their place in the original text I take it from."

So chance procedure? Random juxtaposition? Extreme collage?

"Oh no. I choose each phrase and my editing includes rearranging, re-ordering, replacing lines with others, as any writer does. There is no chance procedure. I choose a theme I wish to explore, or which seems present to me in my studies or reading. I believe I am assembling one possible text from an infinite number of possible texts in the world."

You have very quickly had a number of works published in small press magazines and online journals, and now Broken Sleep Books are publishing your first book. Was that a surprise?

"Yes, of course, but I am delighted, especially with the book. I have found much support from a variety of editors (although of course I have had plenty of rejections), but it is all much simpler than the slow way universities and academia process things. Most editors seem friendly and willing to give advice, as well as a simple yes or no reply to submissions. And I like the different range of magazines available. At X-Peri, for instance, who have just published a sequence of mine, my work sits alongside the strangest, most experimental writing and visuals, whilst at I Am Not A Silent Poet the poem is seen as a revolutionary observation, critique or call to arms. Amethyst Review is a busy online blog publishing work about spirituality in the widest sense; A Restricted View From Under the Hedge is a beautiful paperback magazine. I am amazed at how my work is now available to readers, and it was this that encouraged me to try and find a publisher."

There are more and more small presses springing up, but how did you choose where to send your manuscript?

"Broken Sleep Books was the second publisher I submitted to, and they very quickly accepted my book. I was encouraged by the simple design of their books, the number of women on their list, and their commitment to inclusivity and diversity. It seemed a good place to submit to. I had no idea how new the publisher was! But I am very grateful to the editors there and looking forward to seeing my book."

And what's next for Serena Mayer the poet?

"I am working on a poetry sequence using titles from the artist Joan Miró (although the poems are not about his work) and continuing to submit individual poems to magazines. School is about to begin again, so organising and supporting my daughter must be my main concern for a while. I also have an anthropological trip to undertake before Christmas and will have to write that up. I am enjoying creative writing very much at the moment."

Theoretical Complexities is available from www.brokensleepbooks.com

Jonathan Stubbs is a systems analyst in London and an avid reader and cyclist.

NIGEL KENT

Talking To Maggie Sawkins

I met Maggie Sawkins at a poetry workshop in November 2017. At the end of a hard day of activities in an unbearably hot room and with the bar beckoning, Maggie agreed to finish the session by reading us the eponymous poem from her collection, Zones of Avoidance, an intensely personal piece, which explores the effects of addiction on the lives of addicts and their loved ones. When she finished reading, unusually there was no polite, ritual applause and no one moved. There was just silence: the silence of a group of aspiring poets, deeply moved, who ironically could not find words (or any other appropriate vehicle) to express what they were feeling. At that moment I understood what Emily Dickinson meant when she said:
"If I read a book and it makes my whole body so cold no fire can ever warm me, I know that is poetry."

Maggie's work is frequently anthologised and she has published three poetry collections: *Charcot's Pet* (Flarestack, 2003); *The Zig Zag Woman* (Two Ravens Press, 2007) and *Zones of Avoidance* (Cinnamon Press, 2015). The publication of her new chapbook, *Many Skies have Fallen,* is due at the time of writing and will be published by Wild Mouse Press.Her poems often explore painful, human situations in an uncompromising and authentic way. However, at the heart of her work is an empathetic, profoundly humane perspective that makes her poetry consistently optimistic no matter how bleak the subject matter.
I caught up with Maggie a year later to find out a little more about her writing.

Can you remember your first poem? What was it about?
"I'd been writing poems since I was about nine years old but my first attempt at writing something serious was when I was thirteen. It was called The Roses and included words that I'd found while reading the dictionary -- the only interesting book we had in our house. It went something like this:

> The red roses stand against the azure sky
> their ethereal beauty suffocates the summer ...

Feeling quite pleased with my efforts I took the poem into school to show my English teacher but unfortunately, he didn't believe that I'd written it. I had an inkling I might be onto something after that. Poetry is something that I've been attracted to from a young age. It probably began with an enjoyment of nursery rhymes and TV adverts and progressed from there. I've always loved reading which has fed into the type of poetry that I write. I guess I learnt from an early age that poetry was something I could do on my own, and it was free."

When I read some of your poems I think of Wordsworth' definition of poetry as "the spontaneous overflow of powerful feelings: it takes its origin from emotion recollected in tranquillity". Would that be a fair reflection of the content and process of your poems?
"I don't recognise myself as a person who "spontaneously overflows with powerful feelings" in the way I conduct myself normally. I probably turned to writing in the first place more to get in touch with how I feel. Writing a poem for me is a process of digging. You have to keep scribbling through the false-starts, falsehoods, inanities, before you get anywhere near to the nub of truth. When you've hit that place, you know it because it has the power to move you. As Robert Frost said, "No tears in the writer, no tears in the reader." As an antidote I sometimes turn to the OuLiPo school of writing which rejects spontaneous chance and the subconscious as sources of literary creativity. However, I tend to keep these poems to myself. I don't think they would be of much value to a reader because they lack emotion."

When you write, do you have an 'ideal audience' in mind?
"When I'm involved in the process of writing the only reader I'm
conscious of is myself. I'm constantly reading and revising as I go along.
If what I've written excites me or moves me, or ideally both, then I'll take
a chance on sending it out into the publishing world."

*I'm often intrigued by your choice of titles, such as 'Poem Composed
While Doing a Headstand', 'Antartica to Tamazipan' and, of course,
'The Zig-Zag Woman'. Can you talk a little about the importance of titles
and what makes a good title?*
"I think it's wise to be wary of the first title that pops into your head.
Sometimes however, especially if you've been living with your poem for a
while, a brilliant title pushes its way up from your sub-conscious.
A poor title is one where it's obvious that the writer hasn't given any
thought to it, one which relies on cliché, or is trite. Long titles have been
trendy for a while and can be interesting, but there's the danger of
appearing gimmicky.
The title of my second collection, The Zig Zag Woman was inspired by
the magic trick where a woman is divided into thirds so that her middle
appears to be displaced to one side. The trick symbolised a point in my
life where I felt I had displaced my heart in order to survive. I rarely
think of a title first. An exception is Bronzefield, a poem in which I
meditate on the origins of the name of a prison, a place where my
daughter spent some time for drug related offences.
The poet Kathryn Simmonds has a very good essay on titles in the
Magma poetry magazine."

*Many poetry readers will associate you with the poem, 'Zones of
Avoidance', for which you won the 'Ted Hughes Award for New Work
in Poetry 2013'. Can you tell us a little about the poem?*
"I'd been reading about walls, searching for a metaphor for what I'd
become. The largest known superstructure in the universe, I discovered,
is the 'Coma Wall', situated 200 million light years away and stretching
beyond the 'Zone of Avoidance'. When you're affected by someone in
the grip of addiction there seems to be only two options – one, the most

natural is to try and rescue; the other is to cut yourself off, demonise the person you love, transform yourself into a wall.

The long poem sequence 'Zones of Avoidance' is an integral part of a live literature production, a multi-media piece deploying film, voices, and sound. The sequence was written over a period of 18 months and was inspired by my personal and professional involvement with people in recovery from addiction. The production combines my own testimony with the voices of addicts in recovery.

The story is very personal. I'd been gathering draft material on the subject over a period of 20 years. Much of it was in the form of diary entries and some was in the form of unsent letters to my grandson, who's been estranged from my daughter since the age of three. My motivation was to keep a record for him – when someone close to you is gripped by addiction you're always expecting the knock on the door. I considered writing the story as a memoir. However, reading back through the drafts, I realised that the 'truth' could be told in relatively few words. Writing in poetry enabled me to tease out the terrible beauty from what, in reality, had been a much darker story.

The dramatic material provided by living in a battlefield is a gift for any writer. I couldn't have made anything up that would have been as fascinating as the reality. I had qualms at first about making the personal so public, but once I found the courage to surrender to the story there was no turning back. My aim as a writer was to find a way of transforming the local into the universal. Including testimonies from recovering addicts and my research into psychoactive substances enabled me to achieve this. The feedback after early performances was overwhelming. Obviously when you've been working on something for so long, you don't know how audiences are going to react. I'm more than delighted that the performance appeals to ordinary people, as well as those already into poetry."

Although many of your poems are often deeply moving, there is also humour in your work. What part does humour play in your poems?
"Life's pretty absurd at times isn't it? I wrote a poem once about how, in the space of one week, three members of my family phoned to tell me

they intended to kill themselves (none of them did!). I wasn't feeling too good myself at the time. Sometimes life's grim. Seeing the funny side of things helps you to survive. I've always been attracted to existentialist writers, such as Camus, who thought that individuals should embrace the absurd condition of human existence while continuing to explore and search for meaning."

I believe you have a new chapbook in production. What can we expect?
"Yes, the chapbook is called 'Many Skies Have Fallen' which is from a quotation by D H Lawrence: "We've got to live, no matter how many skies have fallen." The book contains poems written as a response to the tragic death of my younger daughter's partner, Janusz Jasicki, who drowned in the River Shannon in October 2017. Others, written while Janusz was still alive, are included because they relate to my Irish heritage or because they seem to contain a presentiment not apparent at the time of writing."

Finally, poets owe a debt to the other poets we have read. Who are your favourite poets and what are you reading at the moment?
"After winning a book token for gaining the top CSE grade in English, I went along to our local bookshop in Havant and discovered that there were other poets out there. I came away with 'Selected Poems of Emily Dickinson', 'Selected Poems of John Clare' and Michael Horovitz's 'Children of Albion' anthology. Emily Dickinson has stood the test of time; I didn't get on so well with John Clare, though I gave it a good try. 'Children of Albion' was useful in that it introduced me to contemporary poetry – interestingly, I've only recently noticed that out of the 63 poets included, only 3 of them were women.
When I was thirty I took an A Level in English Literature and studied the metaphysical poets. I particularly liked John Donne – 'Nocturnal on St Lucy's Day' is one of my favourite poems. Studying English at degree level introduced me to the world of contemporary women poets. I was particularly drawn to Sylvia Plath, Adrienne Rich and Anne Sexton.
I also love novels: stories that whisk you away to another country, especially those countries that I'll probably never get the opportunity to

visit. At the moment I'm into Rohinton Mistry. I've just finished reading 'A Fine Balance' and have now moved onto 'Family Matters'. It's set in Bombay and tells the story of an elderly Parsi widower who is beset with Parkinson's disease. Mistry is a wonderfully humane writer. I've learnt so much about Indian history, its politics and its people from reading his novels.

Among poets that I enjoy reading now are Selima Hill, Anne Carson, Louise Gluck, Simon Armitage, W S Graham, Fred Voss, Carolyn Forche ... I have a vast bookshelf! Lately I've been dipping into *A River dies of Thirst*, the last diary of Palestinian poet, Mahmoud Darwish. I've had the book for a while but am revisiting it because I'm currently working on a poetry project with asylum seekers in Portsmouth. I wanted to read something that brought me closer to the experience of people who are estranged from their own country."

Thank you, Maggie.

BARRY TEBB

Warf and Weft is Still Alive and Kicking

When I grew up in the north during the forties and fifties, cotton mills abounded. I had an aunt who worked all her life in one, but now Keighley – once a centre for the spinning industry – struggles to maintain its last two.
While cotton remains a staple of the fabrics in our clothing, most of it is from Asia, especially from Bangladesh, notorious for its sweated labour.

The production standards of this colourful anthology are very high and the illustrations lavish.

The opening poem is a translation of a poem by the weaver-saint Kabir; the translation from Hindi is by Tagore at his best:

The woman who is parted from her lover spins at the spinning wheel. The city of the body arises in its beauty; and within it the palace of the mind has been built.

Debjani Chatterjee's 'Draupadi's Sari' retells a tale from the Mahabharata epic. The five Pandava brothers were cheated at dice and enslaved. Their common wife Draupadi too was staked enslaved and dragged into a royal court where an attempt was made to strip her in public. But the attempt was foiled by the intervention of Krishna, who miraculously transforms her sari into a never-ending garment.

Though none could see Krishna,
all witnessed a wonder.
Draupadi's inner eye
viewed the Lord's kindly hand;
others – her endlessly streaming sari.

115

The incident reminds me of Homer's depiction of Odysseus' wife Penelope fending off suitors by weaving a shroud for Laertes by day and then unpicking her stitches by night.

In a brief compass of forty-four pages lies an assortment of many-hued poems by writers as diverse as Brian D'Arcy, Rashida Islam and Alexandra Carr Malcolm, and it is a tribute to the editor that she was able to collate such an exquisite tapestry within such parameters.

The book flooded my mind with my own memories – especially of the eighteenth-century weaver's cottage where Brenda Williams and I lived in 1967. Situated in the hamlet of Honley outside Huddersfield, the cottage had as many windows as the walls could contain to sustain the handloom weavers in their craft where light was at a premium. Alongside the cottage lay a tarmac road, but it had – in perfect condition – a pack-horse road used by the weavers to transport their wares to the cloth halls. An abiding memory – as is this anthology.

Spinning a Yarn: Weaving a Poem ed. Debjani Chatterjee, Sahitya Press and the University of Nottingham, 2018, ISBN: 13 9780853583233, £4

THEY SAY, WRITE ABOUT
WHAT YOU KNOW
BUT I DON'T KNOW
ANYTHING.

postcards from the hedge
@mooseallain